ROCK & ROLL
HALL OF FAMERS

The Beach Boys

MARK HOLCOMB

the rosen publishing group's
rosen
central

For Jacki

Published in 2003 by The Rosen Publishing Group, Inc.
29 East 21st Street, New York, NY 10010

Copyright © 2003 by The Rosen Publishing Group, Inc.

First Edition

Library of Congress Cataloging-in-Publication Data

Holcomb, Mark.
The Beach Boys / by Mark Holcomb.— 1st ed.
p. cm. — (Rock & roll hall of famers)
Includes bibliographical references (p.   ) and discography (p.   ).
ISBN 0-8239-3643-0
1. Beach Boys—Juvenile literature. 2. Rock musicians—United
States—Biography—Juvenile literature. [1. Beach Boys. 2. Musicians.]
I. Title. II. Series.
ML3930.B37 H68 2002
782.42166'092'2–dc21

2001007010

Manufactured in the United States of America

CONTENTS

The Beach Boys are still one of the most beloved and acclaimed bands in rock and roll history.

Introduction

When you think of the Beach Boys, chances are you picture surfboards, hot rods, and the warm beaches of sunny southern California. What you may not know is that behind the group's fun-loving image and carefree songs are years of hard work, career ups and downs, and personal tragedy. The Beach Boys are, in both their lives and music, more complicated than they first appear.

Much of the group's talent belongs to Brian Wilson, their lead songwriter, composer, and producer. The other band members—Brian's younger brothers Dennis and Carl, their cousin Mike Love, and high school chum Al Jardine— made significant contributions to the Beach Boys, but it was Brian's inventive way with rhythm and harmony that gave their music its distinctive sound. With songs like "Help Me, Rhonda," "Little Deuce Coupe," and "Good Vibrations," he used surf rock to push popular music into new creative territory. At the same time, his melodies showed the influence of traditional vocal groups like the Four Freshmen, whom he had grown up listening to. Under Brian's guidance, the Beach Boys were the musical link between the innocence of the 1950s and the experimentation of the 1960s.

They were also incredibly successful. From coast to coast—even in places where there was no coast—and around the world, they scored one hit record after another. They were top sellers well into the 1980s, and they remain fan favorites to this day. Even after their album sales began to

Brian Wilson, the main creative force behind the Beach Boys, is pictured here in 1976.

taper off, fans, professional musicians, and rock critics alike acknowledged Brian Wilson as one of rock and roll's true geniuses. With that kind of a track record, what could have possibly gone wrong for the Beach Boys?

Practically everything, it sometimes seems. Their runaway success and the easy southern California lifestyle they helped define eventually became a trap for the band—a trap that not all of them survived. The emotionally fragile Brian took the pressures and indulgences of rock stardom hardest of all, and he spent several years in virtual hiding. As he put it in his 1991 autobiography, *Wouldn't It Be Nice,* "In those days I was content to live inside myself, a withdrawn mass of misery and confusion and fear." In many ways, it's a miracle he survived.

But with the help of family and friends, and through his own determination, Brian Wilson overcame his fears and addictions. He no longer performs with the Beach Boys, but he is finally a happy and healthy man. Long before this hard-won contentment, however, there was the band: five southern California teenagers with a love of fast cars, perfect waves, and, most of all, rock and roll music.

WHEN I GROW UP (TO BE A MAN)

Hawthorne, California, is five miles from the nearest beach. Nevertheless, this conservative, working-class suburb south of Los Angeles is where the Beach Boys first found their musical inspiration. Among its blocks of modest stucco tract houses with postage-stamp sized lawns, Brian, Dennis, and Carl Wilson, Mike Love,

and Al Jardine nurtured the one-of-a-kind sound that would take the world by storm, and make them, for better and worse, rock and roll legends.

California Saga

When Brian and Dennis were born, on June 20, 1942, and December 4, 1944, respectively, the Wilsons lived even farther from the ocean. Their parents, Murry and Audree, had rented a cramped apartment near downtown Los Angeles shortly after they were married in 1938. Murry, who was originally from Hutchinson, Kansas, had moved with his family to southern California as a young boy. His father, William (nicknamed Bud), was an unsuccessful, hard-drinking plumber who frequently took out his frustrations on his wife, Edith, and their eight children. Murry told his sons that he'd been abused by Bud as a child, but that he also had happier memories of singing and playing piano with his parents and siblings long into the night.

In 1945, Murry and Audree bought a house on 119th Street and Kornblum Avenue in

Hawthorne—the "City of Good Neighbors" as it was called at the time. Murry had steady work at the Goodyear Tire and Rubber Company (where he'd lost an eye a few years before in a freak accident) and later at his own company, ABLE Machinery. Carl was born on December 21, 1946, and the Wilson family was complete.

The best thing about the new house, at least from Brian's perspective, was a converted garage that Murry had turned into the family music room. It contained a phonograph (or record player), a piano, and an organ. The boys listened night after night as their mother and father happily performed duets of the latest popular songs and a few of Murry's own compositions. Murry was an amateur songwriter who had hoped for a big break his entire life. His only real success, though, came when a local group called the Bachelors recorded his song "Two Step Side Step." Bandleader Lawrence Welk later performed the tune on his weekly live radio show. (Brian remembers his father being so overcome with emotion during the broadcast that he left the room.) Murry continued to

In 1966, the Beach Boys were at their peak, both in terms of commercial success and critical acclaim.

write songs long after the Beach Boys had become a worldwide sensation, and he even released an album called *The Many Moods of Murry Wilson* in 1967.

"Rock and Roll Music"

As the years passed and the Wilson brothers grew older, they seemed like most other southern California teenage boys. Brian and Dennis were handsome, popular athletes at Hawthorne High School, and Carl was their shy, likable kid brother. But the boys had a secret they rarely talked about with each other, let alone with friends or strangers.

Murry, despite his own history of abuse, routinely mistreated his children. As the oldest, Brian was a frequent target of his father's rage, and he responded by becoming withdrawn and fearful of social contact. But the independent and willful Dennis took most of Murry's abuse. As Brian recalled, "Dennis . . . was forever on the short end of my dad's extremely short fuse." While Dennis rebelled by spending long periods away from home, often getting into trouble, Brian had his own way of dealing with the pain.

From the time he was eight years old, Brian—who had supposedly hummed the "Marine Corps Hymn" at just eleven months old—loved music. As a youngster, he had written his first song on a toy ukulele. Later, he took accordion lessons, but he soon frustrated his teacher by refusing to learn how to read music; he played perfectly by ear. The lessons stopped when Brian outgrew his child-sized accordion, but by then he had become fascinated with the piano in the Wilson music room.

The first time he sat down to play, the experience was "pure happiness." He said, "For the first time, I was in touch with the deep waters of my soul." He continued to teach himself how to play by observing his father, also a self-taught pianist, or by playing along to records. "I was obsessed," he later said. "Music was a compulsion, as necessary to my health and well-being as food and sleep." This obsession was fueled by the Four Freshmen, a vocal group he heard one morning on Audree's car radio whose four-part harmonies captured Brian's imagination.

The Four Freshmen, who began as a barbershop quartet, were moderately successful during the late '50s and early '60s. Their gentle, intricate melodies were Brian's first model for the tunes that would make the Beach Boys famous. At night, he gathered his family in the music room and taught them how to harmonize to albums by the Freshmen and another group called the Hi-Los. With a tape recorder he'd received for his sixteenth birthday, he even began recording songs of his own. Carl accompanied him on a guitar he'd learned to play from a neighbor, and Dennis—a fledgling drummer—sometimes joined in. Later, Carl introduced Brian to the joys of R & B, courtesy of DJ Johnny Otis's nine-to-midnight radio show on KFOX. There was no turning back: The Wilson brothers were officially hooked on rock and roll.

Family Affair

As he neared high school graduation, Brian signed up for academic courses at El Camino Junior College in nearby Lawndale. His heart,

The band relaxes during a
quiet moment in nature.

however, was in his piano playing, singing, and songwriting. In fact, he had moved his bed into the Wilson home's music room in order to be closer to his beloved piano. What got him thinking seriously about a music career, however, was the encouragement of his cousin Mike Love.

Mike, the oldest child of Murry's sister Emily and her husband, Milton, was a self-assured young man a few years older than Brian. Although his father owned a successful

Fun Fact!

The only Beach Boy who actually knew how to surf was Dennis Wilson. The extended family's most accomplished surfer, however, was Stephen Love, Mike's brother and later the group's business manager. Brian Wilson, who feared the ocean, was finally coaxed onto a surfboard for a 1976 TV special called *The Beach Boys: It's O.K.*

sheet-metal factory and the Love family was financially comfortable, Mike lacked direction. He worked for his father during the day and pumped gas by night, with few other prospects on the horizon. Already married and a father himself, he wanted more from his life, and he recognized an opportunity in Brian's gift for music. The two had sung together since childhood, most notably at family holiday get-togethers, and it was a pastime they both enjoyed. After Brian graduated, Mike persuaded him to spend his spare time singing and writing songs.

Not long after, Brian bumped into an old high school acquaintance named Alan Jardine on the El Camino College campus. Like Brian, Al was an athlete with a love of music. He played guitar and bass and had his own folk group called the Islanders. The two got to talking, and Brian invited Al to his house to sing with him, Mike, Dennis, and Carl.

The group was so excited by the sounds they made together that they soon rented guitars, amps, drums, and an upright bass for a weekend

Early in their career, the Beach Boys possessed an all-American, clean-cut image that epitomized Southern California culture.

jam session. Murry and Audree were on vacation at the time, and Brian spent the food money they'd left for the boys on the instruments and equipment. The results were encouraging—even to the raging Murry, who returned home to find his music room looking more like a makeshift studio. He agreed to contact a couple he knew in the recording industry on behalf of the soon-to-be Beach Boys.

Surf City Soul

Hite and Dorinda Morgan owned Guild Music, a mom-and-pop music publishing business on Melrose Avenue in Hollywood. They'd published Murry's "Two Step Side Step" several years earlier, and they felt obligated to listen to the band his sons had formed. The boys had decided on the group name the Pendletones—a reference to the Pendleton-brand plaid flannel shirts popular at the time—and played a traditional folk song called "Sloop John B" for the occasion. (Five years later, Brian would include the track on the Beach Boys' album *Pet Sounds*.)

The Morgans, while impressed with the five hopeful teenagers' obvious talent, were unexcited by the song. Brian remembers Hite telling them, "These days you need something original. You gotta have an angle. The music business is all about selling a product." Thinking quickly, Dennis began telling the Morgans about surfing and the surf crowd he hung out with. He even said that Brian had written a surfing tune. The couple was interested and told the boys to go practice the song and call them when they were ready for another audition. Brian, who had started writing a tune called "Surfin'" while still in high school, was determined to finish the song. Back home, he elaborated on the basic melody while Mike hit upon the chorus in a moment of inspiration. This was to be the beginning of an on-again, off-again songwriting partnership that would last for over thirty years.

When the Pendletones returned to perform "Surfin'" for the Morgans a few days later, Hite had just three words to say: "That's a smash!"

What's in a Name?

Within a few weeks, the group was at Keen Studios in Beverly Hills to record "Surfin'." Carl

The band poses shortly after their arrival at a London airport in November 1969.

and Brian played guitar, Al was on bass, and all five boys were slated to sing. There was only one hitch: Brian and Carl didn't think Dennis was a good enough drummer and had brought along a session player to fill in for him. Dennis was furious, but the Morgans ended up not using his replacement, either; according to Carl, Brian simply pounded on the lid of a handy garbage can for the record's percussion effects! After a dozen or so takes, the record was finally cut.

The Morgans, with whom the group had signed a publishing contract, arranged for a small local label called Candix to release "Surfin'." On December 8, 1961, it was delivered to record stores throughout the western states. Copies also showed up at on the Wilsons' doorstep, where the family was shocked to discover that the Pendletones had been renamed the Beach Boys. A young promotion man at Candix thought the group's new name would sell more records, and despite Murry's objections, there wasn't enough money to repress and repackage the discs. The band was stuck with the name.

"Surfin'" debuted on Los Angeles radio station KFWB at number thirty-three on December 29. Dennis recalled hearing it for the first time while he and his brothers cruised in Brian's car. "Nothing will ever top the expression on Brian's face," he said. Dennis began shouting excitedly to anyone who would listen that they were on the radio, while Carl celebrated by drinking as many milkshakes as he could. Despite a predictably critical response from Murry, the Beach Boys knew they were on their way.

1961
The Pendletones—Brian, Dennis, and Carl Wilson, Mike Love, and Al Jardine—record "Surfin'" for Hite and Dorinda Morgan. The record is released by Candix on December 8.

1964
"I Get Around" becomes the group's first number-one record. The Beach Boys tour Australia and Europe for the first time. Brian and Marilyn Rovell are married.

1965
Bruce Johnston joins the group when Brian stops touring. *The Beach Boys Today!* and *Summer Days (And Summer Nights!!)* are released.

1962
The Beach Boys sign with Capitol Records, which releases the Beach Boys' first album, *Surfin' Safari*, in October. The group tours the United States for the first time that summer.

1966
Pet Sounds is released in May. Capitol also releases *The Best of the Beach Boys*, and "Good Vibrations" reaches number one on the charts.

1968
The Beach Boys release *Wild Honey*, and Mike becomes a lifelong follower of the Maharishi Mahesh Yogi.

1973
Endless Summer, a top-selling greatest-hits compilation, is released. The Beach Boys are named Band of the Year by *Rolling Stone* magazine.

1976
The Beach Boys' *15 Big Ones* hits number five on the *Billboard* charts.

1971
Dennis stars in *Two-Lane Blacktop*. The Beach Boys release *Surf's Up*, which reaches number twenty-nine on the charts.

1988
The Beach Boys are inducted into the Rock and Roll Hall of Fame. Their song "Kokomo" becomes a number-one hit. Brian releases his first solo album.

CATCH A WAVE

"Surfin'" took off on the local singles charts like wildfire and hit *Billboard*'s number seventy-five spot by March 1962. This convinced the Beach Boys that they were a real rock and roll band. Brian and Mike (who had quit both of his jobs) wrote dozens of new songs, including "Surfer

Girl" and "Surfin' Safari," which the group recorded with the Morgans at Keen Studios. Murry, who had assumed the position of band manager, tirelessly promoted the group by calling radio stations around the country. He even booked the band's first gigs at local rock clubs.

"Two Step Side Step"

Bad news arrived when the "Surfin'" royalty check showed up from Candix: It was for less than $1,000, to be split five ways. The Wilsons and Mike were bitterly disappointed, and Al, who had been preparing to study dentistry, quit the band. "You've got to understand," he told a stunned Brian, "it's not working for me." Murry quickly hired a thirteen-year-old friend of Dennis's named David Marks to replace Al on their upcoming tour. At Murry's insistence, David took over for Brian on rhythm guitar while Brian reluctantly switched to bass.

Around that time, Brian met fellow musician and Beach Boys fan Gary Usher. The two hit it off right away and began working on songs together. They cowrote "The Lonely Sea" and "409," the Beach Boys' first hot-rod song, as well as the moody "In My Room," which described the sense of peace Brian felt in his music room. The two boys enjoyed writing together, but Murry was suspicious of Gary's motives. He resented the time Brian spent with Gary, and he did his best to break up the friendship. In the end, he succeeded: Gary and Murry came to blows during a recording session for the group's first album, and Brian sided with his dad. It would be years before Brian and Gary would meet again.

Murry managed to interest Capitol Records executive Nick Venet in the Beach Boys. Unhappy with the group's commitment to the Morgans, Murry had the group rerecord a handful of Brian and Mike's new songs at Western Studios and brought them to Capitol for Venet to hear. The young A&R man flipped, particularly over "Surfin' Safari." "Before eight bars had spun around, I knew it was a hit record," Venet later said. "I knew the song was going to change West Coast music." It would definitely change the Beach Boys' lives: Capitol agreed to release the songs and later offered them a recording contract. Murry quickly formed his own music publishing company, Sea of Tunes, to secure the rights to all Beach Boys songs.

Capitol released "409" in June 1962. To the group's disappointment, the song received little airplay. But once Capitol began plugging its B-side, "Surfin' Safari," both tunes became hits—"Safari" eventually climbed to number fourteen on the charts. Capitol wanted an album to back up the record's success.

Surfin' Safari was recorded during several long sessions and released on October 1, 1962. It didn't generate as much enthusiasm as the singles, due in part to the record company's rush to get it out, but it still reached number thirty-two on the album charts by Thanksgiving. Murry contacted KFWB disc jockey Roger Christian, a car buff who had praised "409" on the air, and set up a meeting between Brian and the DJ. The two were soon writing songs together, with Roger filling the void left by Gary Usher's departure.

The Beach Boys pose backstage during a show at the Finsbury Astoria in London, England.

Breaking Away

The Beach Boys embarked on their first tour of the United States in the summer of 1962, traveling together in a cramped station wagon. Mike, David, Carl, and Dennis loved the freedom of being away from home, but for Brian it was an obstacle to writing songs. To make matters worse, Murry, who accompanied the group on some of their early gigs, established an elaborate "fine" system in which the boys forfeited pay for swearing or talking to girls. Even though the group members easily got around Murry's restrictions (especially when he didn't tour with them), the arrangement made life on the road as miserable for the rest of the band as it was for Brian.

Fans and music industry insiders alike were beginning to take notice of Brian's good looks and musical talent, and in some ways this made up for his troubled home life. So did his girlfriend, Judy Bowles, the blond-haired, blue-eyed inspiration for many of his early songs. But as Brian became more committed to his music career, he had less time to devote to Judy, and the relationship ended. Even worse, Murry's incessant nagging was becoming too much for the emotionally fragile Brian to handle. He moved out of the Wilsons' Hawthorne home shortly after *Surfin' Safari* was released. He roomed for a while with a young University of Southern California student named Bob Norberg.

Around this time, Brian met teenaged sisters Marilyn and Diane Rovell at a Beach Boys

Bruce Johnston, an accomplished singer, piano player, and record producer, joined the Beach Boys in 1965.

show at Pandora's Box, a popular underage club on Hollywood's Sunset Strip. He was soon smitten with both girls and began spending a lot of time at their parents' house in the Fairfax district of Los Angeles. Irving and Mae Rovell were gentle, tolerant people who indulged Brian and encouraged his songwriting. Their household was as soothing and supportive as Murry and Audree's was tense and demeaning, so Brian and the rest of the Beach Boys made it an unofficial group hangout. Brian also wrote and produced a few songs for the Rovell sisters and their cousin Ginger Blake, who recorded under the name the Honeys, but the group failed to score on the charts. Brian's affections swung between Marilyn and Diane—and even their younger sister, Barbara—for years to come, but it was Marilyn he turned to for companionship when he finally moved out on his own.

"Loop De Loop"

Capitol released the Beach Boys' "Surfin' U.S.A." and "Shut Down" (the latter with lyrics by Roger Christian) in March 1963. Both songs charted, and "Surfin' U.S.A." became the group's first song to crack the top ten. Capitol rushed them into the studio to record their second album, *Surfin' U.S.A.*, which included five instrumental tracks to fill the space between singles. As with *Surfin' Safari,* Nick Venet produced the album, but this time he allowed Brian more freedom over the production process. For the next single, "Surfer Girl," he even let Brian record at Western Studios instead of Capitol's in-house facility. The song, Brian's first as producer, was an instant hit. So was its flip-side, "Little Deuce Coupe," and Capitol demanded another album to capitalize on the singles' success. *Surfer Girl* was released less than a month after *Surfin' U.S.A.*, and it revealed Brian's growing skill as a producer, songwriter, and composer. *Surfer Girl* stayed on the charts for nearly a year, topping at number seven.

The Beach Boys were on a roll, and the shortsighted Capitol wanted them to record as much material as possible before the surf craze died out. Yet another album, *Little Deuce Coupe*, was released in November 1963. "There was no rest," Brian wrote in his 1991 autobiography. "It was always more, more, more." Still, he was moving the group away from their reliance on surf songs and was learning the sophisticated studio techniques that would soon make him famous.

Meanwhile, Murry Wilson signed the group to the William Morris Agency for their second United States tour. The band was a huge attraction wherever they played, but Brian hated

Did You Know?

Chuck Berry is listed as cowriter of the Beach Boys' first top-ten hit, "Surfin' U.S.A." Berry's music publishers, Arc Music, claimed in a lawsuit that the song used the melody from his "Sweet Little Sixteen," and Capitol Records settled the case out of court by giving Berry a writer's credit on Brian and Mike's song. Brian claims that the similarity was unintentional.

touring more than ever. "The truth was I simply couldn't write on the road . . . If I didn't write, I didn't function properly. I was wracked with worry and anxiety." He began missing dates and showing up late for performances, and he started drinking to calm his jangled nerves. Murry was forced to rehire Al Jardine for the remainder of the tour to make up for Brian's unreliability. The recently married Al, whose studies hadn't gone well, also began recording with the band again, and Murry took the opportunity to fire the boisterous David Marks.

Fun, Fun, Fun in Europe

In 1964, the Beach Boys' growing fame was eclipsed by the enormous popularity of the Beatles. Brian admired their records but felt intimidated by their hip sophistication. It didn't help that the release of the Beatles' number-one "I Want to Hold Your Hand" coincided with that of the Beach Boys' "Fun, Fun, Fun," which charted at number fifteen.

The group was busy putting the finishing touches on their next album, *Shut Down Volume 2,*

The band poses with a dragster in London's West End during a 1964 tour.

to be followed by a tour of Australia—their first outside the United States. Everyone except Brian was overjoyed at the prospect of seeing another part of the world. He and Marilyn argued before the band's flight out, which caused Brian to suffer even more on the tour. The Beach Boys were a smash Down Under, however, and Brian decided that he would ask Marilyn to marry him once he returned home. They were wed in a modest civil service in Los Angeles, after an earlier attempt in Las Vegas failed when Brian forgot to bring his birth certificate.

Despite the threat from the Beatles, 1964 was the Beach Boys' best year yet. *Shut Down Volume 2* and its follow-up, *All Summer Long*, were released. The latter featured the group's first number-one single, "I Get Around," as well as the top-ten hit "When I Grow Up (To Be a Man)," which charted at number nine. The band appeared on *The Ed Sullivan Show* in September, causing almost as much of a frenzy as the Beatles had on the same show in February. Finally, they took off for their first-ever European tour in October.

While European fans were even wilder about the Beach Boys than the Australians had been, Brian was under more pressure than ever. He had recently fired Murry from his position as band manager, and even though he was finally free from his father's constant bickering, he felt guilty over their subsequent estrangement. Brian was also as depressed as ever over not being able to work on new songs, and he quickly became undependable. He broke down in a club in Copenhagen, Denmark, and had to be escorted back to his hotel room by a concerned Dennis and Carl. On the flight home from the tour, Brian decided it was time he stopped touring altogether. He dreaded telling his band mates, but at that point none of them could know that his dedication to writing and recording would result in the most critically acclaimed album of their career.

GOOD VIBRATIONS

The Beach Boys finished off 1964 with a bang. A live album, *Beach Boys Concert*, was released in October and shot to number one on the charts—a first for the group. The top-selling *The Beach Boys' Christmas Album* hit record stores the same month, and the band was slated for a brief

tour of the western United States before the holiday season. Brian and Marilyn moved to a larger apartment in West Hollywood, and even carefree ladies' man Dennis showed signs of settling down.

Turbulent Times

The bliss was quickly interrupted, however. Mike divorced his wife, Francine, not long after the European tour wrapped up, and Murry and Audrec separated later that year. Even worse, Brian suffered a panic attack on a plane to Houston, Texas, as the group set off on their latest tour. He was overcome with anxiety about his marriage, which was becoming troubled, and his competition with other bands. Carl and Dennis sat with him until the plane landed, and Brian was taken to a doctor. He left the tour early and returned home to L.A., where Audree picked him up at the airport. She recalled, "He was in a bad state, crying; then he stopped and talked a lot." Brian told his mom about his decision to stop touring. When the rest of the group returned, he gathered them in the studio and broke the news. The Beach Boys would go on, he said, but as two separate units: Dennis, Carl, Mike, and Al would perform on the road, and Brian would compose and record at home. They were stunned by his decision. In time, though, they reluctantly agreed to Brian's arrangement.

The Beach Boys tried out the new setup not long after. On a fourteen-day tour of the states, Brian was replaced by guitarist and singer Glen Campbell, an ace session musician. Campbell stayed with the group for three months, but left to pursue a successful solo career. As a parting gift, Brian produced Campbell's first single, "Guess I'm Dumb," with the Honeys on backup vocals.

The year 1965 started promisingly for the band. Their seventh album, *The Beach Boys Today!*, was released in March. It spawned five hit singles, including "Do You Wanna Dance" (featuring Dennis on lead vocals) and the number-one "Help Me, Rhonda." The songs were slower and more thoughtful than on previous Beach Boys' albums,

Mike Love holds a platinum record the band received for selling a million copies of an album.

as Brian was finally able to relax and make the kind of music he, and not Capitol Records, wanted. The company executives and Mike Love were skeptical of the new sound, however, and would become even more so as the year wore on.

To round out the touring group, Mike had hired Bruce Johnston, a singer, piano player, and record producer from Beverly Hills. Bruce first

Bruce Johnston: "I Write the Songs"

Bruce Johnston was already a music industry veteran when he joined the Beach Boys. "I've been recording since 1957," Bruce said in a 1990 interview. "I was in a band with Phil Spector back then; he got sounds that haven't been invented. I backed up Ritchie Valens for three months in 1958, as well." He and Terry Melcher (later a friend of Dennis's) were members of the Rip Chords, a surf band that had a minor hit called "Hey Little Cobra." "We used the same voices under a variety of different names—Bruce and Terry, the Rip Chords, the Rogues. We had chart records under all these names." Bruce and Terry later started their own record label, Equinox.

Aside from his contribution to the Beach Boys, Bruce is best known for penning "I Write the Songs," which was a

smash hit for singer Barry Manilow in 1975. But Bruce first offered the song to teen heartthrob David Cassidy. "I warned him: it might be a hit, and end your career. He said, what do you mean? I said, well, imagine the Rolling Stones selling eight million copies of 'Tie a Yellow Ribbon'! But for Barry Manilow, it was perfect."

played with the Beach Boys during one of Brian's recording sessions in April 1965 and joined them later that month on tour. He became a permanent member of the band after the next tour and appeared on the rest of their albums.

"Don't Worry Baby"

Summer Days (And Summer Nights!!), the Beach Boys' next album, was Bruce's first as a full-

Al Jardine and Bruce Johnston onstage during a concert in London in 1966.

fledged member of the band. Released in summer 1965, it reached number two on the album charts—the Beatles' *Beatles VI* was at the top—and included the number-three single "California Girls." With its gentle symphonic opening and use of overdubbing, the song revealed just how experimental Brian's music was becoming thanks to his newfound freedom in the studio.

This shift was also due in part to his friendship with Loren Schwartz, an assistant at the William Morris Agency he'd met earlier that year. Loren was in tune with the growing countercultural movement in Los Angeles, and introduced Brian to a hipper crowd than he was used to. Unfortunately, marijuana and LSD were a part of the lifestyle that came with that crowd. Eager to escape the pressures of rock and roll stardom and the anxiety he had felt since childhood, Brian indulged in both drugs. Despite the disapproval of Marilyn and the rest of the Beach Boys (except for Dennis, who was developing a drug habit of his own), Brian would abuse substances for years to come.

Brian and Marilyn bought their first home together later that summer. Set in the hills overlooking Hollywood and the San Fernando Valley, the house on Laurel Way became an eccentric haven for Brian, his family, and their revolving group of friends and hangers-on. It came with a pool in which Brian began conducting his business meetings. The couple later installed a full-sized tent in the living room and a playground in the front entry that visitors had to climb through in order to get inside the house.

The festive atmosphere at Laurel Way found its way onto the Beach Boys' next album. Pressured by Capitol to release another live disc, Brian proposed that he and the band, along with a few friends and additional musicians, throw a party at Western Studios and record that instead. The label went for the idea, and *The Beach Boys Party!* was born. The sounds of people talking and laughing can be heard throughout the album, which included rousing versions of pop standards like "Alley Oop" and "Barbara Ann" (which became an unexpected number-two hit), as well as a couple of Beatles tunes. Mike also met his second wife, Suzanne, at the session. She'd been invited to a party but had no idea that it would be in the Beach Boys' studio.

While the project was a lot of fun to produce and participate in, *The Beach Boys Party!* was merely a way for Brian to stall the record company. His real interest was in the upcoming album he'd been planning ever since he stopped touring.

Fun Fact!

Brian's house on Laurel Way featured a huge sandbox surrounding the piano in the music room. Brian claimed that it made him "feel like a little kid" and got his creative juices flowing. It was finally removed when several inches of sand were later discovered inside the piano.

Spiritual Music

While the other Beach Boys were busy performing in early 1966, Brian began putting together songs for what he hoped would be "the greatest rock album ever made." The Beatles' *Rubber Soul* had just been released worldwide, and it was a revelation to Brian and rock and roll fans everywhere. Brian decided he would try to top the Beatles' achievement. His album would contain what he called "spiritual music," revolving around the theme of the loss of innocence.

Loren Schwartz had introduced him to Tony Asher the year before, and Brian discovered that the young ad copywriter also wrote songs. Instead of using his most reliable collaborator, Mike Love, Brian invited Tony to the studio to write the words to his masterpiece. As Mike said in a 1992 interview, "I didn't participate in a lot of the stuff that was going on there, because I just didn't think the psychedelic route was the way to go." (In the end, he did contribute to "Wouldn't It Be Nice" and "I Know There's an Answer.") Despite

Brian's inability to start work before noon, he and Tony finished the songs in just three weeks. The two would discuss ideas for songs during the afternoon, and Tony would go home and write the lyrics overnight. As he put it years later, "The general tenor of the lyrics was always [Brian's] . . . I was really just his interpreter."

Next, Brian hired the top session musicians in Los Angeles to record the backing music for the songs. This featured such diverse instruments as harpsichord, accordion, and theremin (an early type of synthesizer). By the time the rest of the Beach Boys returned home from a tour of Japan, Brian was ready for them to record the vocal tracks. They weren't happy about being made to feel like hired singers, but Brian was persistent. The group sang their parts—including a memorable lead vocal performance by Carl on "God Only Knows"—and Capitol was informed that the album, called *Pet Sounds,* was finished. The title came from a joke Mike had made about how some of the instruments in the album's mix could only be heard by dogs' ears.

The record company was dissatisfied with *Pet Sounds* and feared that it had strayed too far from the Beach Boys' established sound to be successful. Though hardly a failure when released in May 1966, the album didn't sell as many copies as their earlier LPs. It reached number eleven on the album charts, while the singles "Caroline, No" and "Sloop John B" hit number thirty-two and number three respectively. Everyone involved was disappointed, but music critics in the United States and especially England raved about *Pet Sounds.* Even Paul McCartney of the Beatles was a fan. Reminiscing about the first time he heard it, the former Beatle said, "I just thought, 'Oh dear me. This is the album of all time. What are we gonna do?'"

Hoping to recover the group's popularity, Capitol released *The Best of the Beach Boys* compilation only eight weeks after *Pet Sounds.* It was an instant success. Brian was discouraged, but he quickly turned his attention to a song he'd been working on for a few months called "Good Vibrations." This "pocket symphony," as he called it, took seventeen sessions, six weeks, and four studios to record. When "Good Vibrations" was released late that summer, it became the Beach Boys' most successful and best-loved song yet. It was a number-one hit by Christmas.

With this happy occurrence spurring him on, Brian was ready to begin the even more ambitious follow-up to *Pet Sounds*. Finishing the album, however, would prove to be impossible.

THE NEAREST FARAWAY PLACE

Anxious to begin writing songs for his latest project, Brian remembered a witty young folksinger named Van Dyke Parks he had met through a mutual friend. Brian was impressed by Van Dyke's intelligence and way with words, so he hired the young Pennsylvanian as his lyricist.

Brian explained that the album, originally titled *Dumb Angel* (reportedly his nickname for Dennis), would be his "teenage symphony to God."

When Van Dyke first showed up at the house on Laurel Way to begin work, he was shocked by Brian's extravagance. "It wasn't funny," he commented years later, "a grand piano in a sandbox. I found it offensive." Nevertheless, when Brian saw that his collaborator had nothing to get around on except a motorbike, he gave Van Dyke $5,000 so he could buy a car.

"Add Some Music to Your Day"

By late 1966, after hours of writing, composing, and recording demos for over twenty songs, Brian and Van Dyke had the basic tracks for the Beach Boys' next album ready for the studio. Capitol Records, worried that the group hadn't had a radio hit all summer, printed the new album cover and notified the press of a Christmas release date. *Smile*, as the album was now called, was to include such songs as "Heroes and Villains," "Cabin Essence," and "Do You Dig Worms?" The experimental nature of Brian's arrangements and Van Dyke's complex lyrics were influenced by the growing youth movement in the United States and abroad, but they lacked the political awareness and activism central to that movement. They were mostly expressions of Brian's innermost thoughts and fears.

Meanwhile, the touring members of the Beach Boys were drawing bigger crowds than ever thanks to the continuing success of "Good Vibrations." They left on a tour of the midwestern United States, followed by stops in Sweden, central Europe, and Great Britain (where Mike, Dennis, and Carl bought four Rolls-Royce limousines). Early in the tour, Brian grew worried about how "Good Vibrations" would sound performed live, so he flew to Ann Arbor, Michigan, to help the band rehearse. Together for the first time since the *Pet Sounds* sessions, the group spent a long, tiring day going over each of the songs on the set list. Onstage, however, they were thoroughly prepared, and "Good Vibrations" was note-for-note perfect.

Smile, the Beach Boys' follow-up to their legendary *Pet Sounds*, was never completed.

Brian even took a bow after the show and received a standing ovation.

Back home, he continued recording the music for *Smile* at Gold Star Studios. After more than thirty sessions, *Smile* was still not ready for the vocal tracks. Brian was forced to tell Capitol that the album wouldn't make the new release date of January 15, 1967, and the news was not well received. "At that time," Carl remarked in 1983, "it just seemed inconceivable to spend two years on an album. Just think: two years before, they [Capitol] wanted three albums a year."

"Here Comes the Night"

Record company executives weren't the only ones running out of patience—tempers also

Did You Know?

Brian became completely unpredictable during the *Smile* sessions. At one point, with more than a dozen string musicians waiting for him, Brian wouldn't enter the studio—he said the room was full of "bad vibes." When the segment was finally recorded for a song called "Fire," Brian was convinced that it had actually caused fires in the Los Angeles area.

flared when Brian previewed the album's songs to the rest of the Beach Boys. They were particularly upset by the abstract quality of Van Dyke Parks's lyrics, and they confronted him at a later recording session. When Van Dyke refused to explain the meaning of the words to his songs, he was fired from the project.

The group continued to work on *Smile,* but despite an encouraging studio visit from Paul McCartney, the project seemed more confused and less salvageable with each passing day. Brian's drug use had only intensified his anxiety over topping *Pet Sounds,* and Mike, Al, and Carl constantly pressured him not to change the Beach Boys' formula. The final blow came in April, when the Beatles released "Penny Lane" and "Strawberry Fields," two singles from their next album, *Sergeant Pepper's Lonely Hearts Club Band.* Brian considered the songs works of genius that he would never be able to match, and he lost all initiative to finish his album. Finally, on May 2, 1967, Capitol Records announced to the press that *Smile* had been canceled.

Brian, hailed as a musical genius just a year before, was now seen by his record label and American critics as unreliable and self-indulgent. With his confidence shattered, he made another blunder that only encouraged that impression. Earlier in 1967, he had told the organizers of the upcoming Monterey Pop Festival that the Beach Boys would perform at this gathering of rock and roll's brightest stars. But Brian pulled out at the last minute, fearing that the group's music would seem "old-fashioned" compared to the gritty, openly political songs of performers like Jimi Hendrix and the Who. As a result, *Rolling Stone* magazine scolded the band in print, calling them "totally disappointing." Onstage at the festival, Hendrix summed up the mood when he remarked during his scorching set, "You heard the last of surfing music." The Beach Boys' popularity was declining fast.

"I Know There's an Answer"

When Capitol demanded that Brian come up with a single for the summer of 1967, he put

Pet Sounds Remastered

The Beach Boys' acclaimed album *Pet Sounds* was recorded in mono instead of stereo because Brian Wilson is deaf in his right ear. Since stereophonic recordings use two or more audio channels, they duplicate the way music sounds to someone with hearing in both ears. To someone with hearing in only one ear, even stereo sounds like mono, or single-channel audio.
By 1966, most popular recordings took advantage of the newly available stereophonic process, but Brian couldn't tell the difference. *Pet Sounds* was remastered in stereo and rereleased in 1997, but some of the album's most dedicated fans balked. They considered it disrespectful to Brian's original vision.

together a three-minute and thirty-six second version of "Heroes and Villains" from the *Smile* sessions. Originally conceived as a seven-minute epic about the Old West, it was the first Beach Boys record to be released since October 1966. It reached number twelve on the *Billboard* charts in early September 1967, but it disappeared only two weeks later. The band was further humiliated when they hand-delivered the new single to Hollywood radio station KHJ late one night, only to be told by the DJ on duty that it wasn't on the approved playlist. He finally played the song with the approval of the station manager, but by then the Beach Boys' pride had been hurt.

To try and minimize the damage to the group's reputation, Capitol released another compilation that summer called *Best of the Beach Boys—Volume 2*. It stayed on the charts for over twenty weeks, but only reached the number fifty spot. The record company also wanted an album assembled from the wreckage of *Smile*, to be distributed on the Beach Boys' recently founded Brother Records label.

Brian was no longer interested in coming into the studio by then. He and Marilyn had sold the house on Laurel Way and moved into a mansion on Bellagio Road in the upscale Los Angeles neighborhood of Bel Air. To finish the project, a makeshift studio was built in a music room below the Wilsons' bedroom, and work began on what was to be called *Smiley Smile.* Every member of the group participated in the creation of the new album, and it was the first to credit the Beach Boys as producers instead of just Brian Wilson. "*Smiley Smile* was a very simple album to make," Carl later said. "It took a couple of weeks at Brian's house." It was mixed in a single overnight session and released on September 18, 1967. Although the album stayed on the charts for twenty-one weeks, it never broke into the top forty—another first for the Beach Boys. As Carl put it, "It was a bunt instead of a grand slam."

Brian Cools Out, Mike Tunes In

Despite the blows to their career, the Beach Boys experienced a few personal triumphs during

Brian Wilson is joined onstage by his daughters Carnie (left) and Wendy during a benefit concert.

this phase of their lives. Carl married his girlfriend, Annie Hinsche, in February 1966, and the couple moved into Carl's house in Bel Air. Mike and his wife, Suzanne, had two children—Hayleigh in 1966 and Christian in 1968—while Brian and Marilyn became the parents of a baby girl named Carnie on April 29, 1968. Confirmed bachelor Dennis also became a husband and a father: He and Carol Freedman married in 1965, and Dennis adopted her son, Scott. They had a daughter of their own, Jennifer, in 1967.

Al continued to live a quiet life with his wife, Lynda, in Mandeville Canyon, and even Murry and Audree, despite living in different houses, continued to be friends and companions. But the indulgences and uncertainties of rock stardom made domestic life difficult for the members of the group, and before the decade was over both Mike and Dennis would be divorced. Dennis's escalating drug and drinking problem didn't help matters.

Two months after *Smiley Smile*'s release, the band released the R & B–flavored *Wild Honey* on Capitol. Produced by all the Beach Boys, it managed to spawn a top twenty hit, "Darlin'," based on Brian and Mike's 1964 song "Thinkin' 'Bout You Baby." Although the album only reached number twenty-four on the charts, *Wild Honey* became a fan favorite.

To Carl, it was "music for Brian to cool out by," and the eldest Wilson brother's participation in the project was only a fraction of what it had been during the heyday of *Pet Sounds*. "He was still very spaced," Carl noted. To Marilyn, it seemed more serious than that: Brian was becoming more withdrawn, sleeping well past noon and rarely meeting with friends. His drug use also increased. "There was a difference between having fun and having sick fun," she said. "I don't think I really saw, or let myself see that." Brian himself said of the time, "Every day I had less control over my mind . . . each day became more devoted to merely surviving."

The Beach Boys Try TM

In December 1967, the group encountered the Maharishi Mahesh Yogi at a benefit concert in Paris, France. The Maharishi was the leader of a movement known as transcendental meditation, or TM, which had influenced several notable figures in the West, including the Beatles. Dennis, Carl, and especially Mike became devotees of the Maharishi and raved about TM to Brian. Believing that meditation might help him cope with his emotional problems, Brian traveled

For a time, the Maharishi Mahesh Yogi served as a spiritual guide to many musicians, including the Beatles and some of the Beach Boys.

to New York to meet the Maharishi in early 1968. He was unimpressed, however, and the Maharishi's reputation soon soured with many of his followers; three of the Beatles went so far as to publicly denounce TM. Mike remained a disciple despite the scandal, and he traveled to India to study under the Maharishi.

The Beach Boys

The Beach Boys recorded their next album, *Friends*, in the spring of 1968. It revealed the influence of TM as well as Brian's growing lack of interest. He contributed only three songs to the project, one of which summed up his lifestyle at the time: "Busy Doin' Nothing." Only Dennis's classic "Little Bird" lived up to the group's earlier work. Mike convinced the Beach Boys to tour the southern United States with the Maharishi when the album was finished, but it proved to be a disastrous move. Fans were less interested in hearing the Maharishi's long lectures than the Beach Boys' music, so crowds were sparse. Also, civil rights leader Dr. Martin Luther King Jr. was assassinated in Memphis, Tennessee, just as the tour started, and people were understandably more concerned with the aftermath of this tragedy than with the Maharishi's message. When *Friends* was released that summer, it didn't even break the top 100. It was the worst-selling Beach Boys album ever.

Shut Down

The next stage in the Beach Boys' career was as notable for its troubled relationships as for the music the group made together. Brian continued to sink further into his depression and was finally forced to seek help. Every member of the group except for Al divorced at least once more, and the band went through several managers who left them worse off financially. And, strangest of

all, Dennis made friends—and later enemies—with one of the most infamous murderers in American history.

On the brighter side, Brian and Marilyn's second daughter, Wendy, was born in October 1969, and the movie-star handsome Dennis appeared in the film *Two-Lane Blacktop* in 1971. He also met and married Barbara Charren, a young cashier from Indiana, and the couple had two children together. In addition, the Beach Boys added accomplished musicians Ricky Fataar and Blondie Chaplin to their stage lineup to fill in for the absent Brian.

Dennis and the Wizard

In the spring of 1968, as *Friends* languished in record stores, Dennis met a mysterious drifter and songwriter named Charles Manson. This wild-eyed would-be prophet broke into the house Dennis was renting on Sunset Boulevard one night and made himself at home. Manson brought with him a group of young women, and this "family" convinced Dennis to let them stay.

Charlie, or "the Wizard" as Dennis called him, even enlisted the musician's help in recording some songs he had written.

Dennis, who had recently split up with Carol, was fascinated by the magnetic Manson. He let Charlie use his house and possessions as if they were his own, and Manson was soon borrowing cash and cars and demanding that Dennis book studio time for him. Dennis obliged, but he eventually began to fear the unpredictable Manson and his followers. He demanded that they leave his house and even went into hiding for a while. It was the right move: In August 1969, the Manson family murdered the occupants of a house where Dennis's friend Terry Melcher had once lived. Before the brutal slayings, Charlie had threatened Dennis's life, claiming that the Beach Boy hadn't lived up to his promise to get Manson a record deal. The killers were arrested and tried in November of that year, and Charles Manson was sentenced to life in prison.

Despite these horrifying events, one of Charlie's tunes turned up on the Beach Boys'

Carl Wilson performs at a concert in 1970.

next album, which was also their twentieth. Aside from the Manson-penned "Never Learn Not to Love" (originally titled "Cease to Exist"), *20/20* featured "Cabin Essence" and "Time to Get Alone," both left over from *Smile*, a new composition from Brian called "I Went to Sleep," and the lovely "I Can Hear Music," produced by Carl. Described by Bruce as "a very un-Brian album" because of the increased contribution by other members of the band, *20/20* was a commercial failure. The group went on a European tour to support the album, but shortly after returning home they learned that Capitol Records had canceled their contract. The Beach Boys were without a label.

Nick of Time

To make matters worse, Capitol stopped reissuing the group's older albums, which cut off their sizable royalties income. Scrambling to land a new contract, the Beach Boys' financial manager, Nick Grillo, negotiated with the German company Grammophon, who believed an investment in the band to be a sure thing. The deal fell through, however, when Brian was quoted in a British rock newspaper as saying "inside a few months, we won't have a penny in the bank." The Germans backed out, and Grillo was forced to borrow money from bankers to support the extravagant lifestyles of the group members.

Then, in November 1969, Murry—who owned Sea of Tunes outright after Brian had signed over his remaining share—sold the entire catalog of Beach Boys' songs for a cash payment. Brian was devastated: His songs were all that he could count on as his emotions became less stable, and now they would belong to strangers. It was the last straw. As he wrote in *Wouldn't It Be Nice,* "I was beaten. Despondent, I muddled through the daytimes, struggling to drag my body out of bed but losing the struggle more often than not." Murry, convinced that the Beach Boys were finished, considered the $700,000 he made on the deal to be a good profit. Over time, however, the songs would become worth more than $20 million.

Finally, in January 1970, Nick Grillo signed a deal with Warner Brothers Records to distribute the Beach Boys' new material on the Reprise label. The company stipulated that Brian had to be active in the group as its chief composer and producer, but their first album for Reprise, *Sunflower,* featured only one new Brian Wilson tune. The album was released on August 31, and although it never broke the top 100, it was considered by many to be the best all-around Beach Boys album yet. Carl produced its single, "Add Some Music to Your Day," and Bruce's "Dierdre" became a favorite, while Dennis—who Carl said "was at the very height of his creativity"— wrote and sang "Got to Know the Woman" and the powerful "Slip On Through." Better still, the British press raved that the album was "the Beach Boys' *Sergeant Pepper.*" Despite dismal sales, it was a promising start on the new label.

The Rieley Factor

While promoting *Sunflower,* the Beach Boys met DJ and self-proclaimed journalist Jack Rieley.

They were impressed with Rieley's self-assurance and ideas for how the band could improve its image, so they hired him as their manager. He convinced them to play at the Big Sur Folk Festival, where they were a smash, and an extended gig at Los Angeles's hip Whiskey A Go Go club, where they sold out all four nights and even coaxed Brian onstage. Rieley also booked the band on a United States tour that ended with a hugely successful show at New York City's Fillmore, where they played with the Grateful Dead. To everyone's surprise, the Beach Boys seemed to be on their way back up.

Sadly, the ride was short-lived. Rieley, who hadn't been honest about his past, proved to be even less of a businessman than he was a journalist. He did influence the Beach Boys' 1971 comeback album *Surf's Up*, which featured such gems as Bruce's "Disney Girls" and Brian's soulful "Till I Die"; the LP reached number twenty-nine on the charts. But Rieley also convinced the band to move their families and studio to Amsterdam for eight months in 1972 to record *Holland*, the follow-up to that year's disappointing *Carl and the*

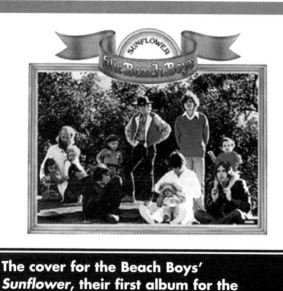

The cover for the Beach Boys' *Sunflower*, their first album for the Reprise label, released in August 1970

Passions—So Tough. In addition, his mismanagement caused Bruce to temporarily leave the group.

Holland was moderately successful and included some noteworthy songs, including the top 100 hit "Sail On, Sailor" (which Warner Brothers hired Van Dyke Parks to help Brian write) and the nostalgic "Mount Vernon and Fairway" (named after the Los Angeles intersection where the Love family home stood). But the album cost Warner Brothers and the Beach Boys a small fortune to make. Jack Rieley was fired shortly after the group returned to the states.

Their next album, 1973's double album *The Beach Boys in Concert,* was yet another commercial failure. But things looked up when a greatest-hits compilation called *Endless Summer* shot up the charts and stayed there for an astonishing seventy-one weeks. Put together by Capitol

Did You Know?

The Beach Boys didn't receive a Grammy Award until 2001. "Good Vibrations" was nominated in 1967 and a *Pet Sounds* box set was up for an award in 1999, but neither work won. Instead, the group was finally honored with a lifetime achievement Grammy forty years after they first got together to play.

Records with Mike's help, it made the Beach Boys famous again. They were even named *Rolling Stone* magazine's Band of the Year for 1973!

"In My Room"

Unknown to the band, Brian had considered suicide while living in Holland. It wasn't the first time: Not long before, he'd dug a "grave" in the backyard of the house on Bellagio Road and fantasized about jumping into it from the roof. He'd also threatened to drive his Rolls-Royce off the Santa Monica Pier. His mental and emotional state hit bottom after returning to California, and his physical condition wasn't far behind. Brian weighed over 200 pounds, ate and drank whatever he pleased, indulged in various drugs, and spent most of his days and nights in bed. He was miserable in every way.

His condition only worsened in the summer of 1973, when Audree called the Wilson brothers to tell them that their father had passed away from a heart attack. Brian, whose complicated love-hate relationship with Murry had troubled

Brian Wilson goofs off with his longtime psychologist, Eugene Landy.

him all his life, was hurt and confused. He began taking even more drugs, including heroin. Fearing for her husband's sanity and the well-being of their children, Marilyn hired Mike's brother Stanley as a live-in caretaker for Brian in 1975; Stephen, Mike's other brother, had taken over the Beach Boys' management by that point. When Stan proved unable to control Brian, Marilyn enlisted the services of celebrity psychologist Eugene Landy.

Dr. Landy, who had also treated rocker Alice Cooper, seemed to be just what Brian needed. His methods were unconventional and his fees sky-high, but by early 1976 he had Brian out of bed and losing weight, resisting drugs, and facing up to reality. By that summer, Brian was even performing again. He was far from rehabilitated, though, and when Warner Brothers, Stephen Love, and the other Beach Boys pushed him back into the studio, he cracked. Landy was called in to help, and his salary shot up even higher. Nevertheless, Brian was able to record with Landy's help. The new record, *15 Big Ones* (which Dennis wanted to call *Group Therapy*) was promoted with a high-profile "Brian Is Back!" campaign, but in truth only half of its songs were Brian Wilson compositions. Even though it wasn't a critical success, the album reached number five on the *Billboard* charts.

New Lows

The more Dr. Landy helped Brian, the farther away the Beach Boys' founder drifted from the rest of the group. Stephen and Mike Love were angry over the psychologist's increasing salary, while the other band members resented his control over Brian. Even Marilyn began to be suspicious of Landy's influence. Around Christmas of 1976, with Brian's questionable consent, Eugene Landy was fired. Stan Love and his friend Rushton "Rocky" Pamplin were hired to keep Brian on track, but they lacked Landy's experience. Instead of building trust with Brian, they intimidated him—and, Brian later claimed, physically and emotionally abused him as well. They managed to keep him off drugs and in the studio for a while, but it wasn't long before Brian was back to his old habits.

Around that time, the Beach Boys were signed to the CBS label. They were under tremendous pressure to live up to this lucrative new contract: Their final Warner Brothers LP, *The Beach Boys Love You*, failed to generate any chart action when it was released in April 1977, and CBS executives had begun to have second thoughts. Instead of pulling together, though, the band splintered. Mike flew to Switzerland to be with the Maharishi, Dennis booked studio time for a solo album, and Brian retreated to his bedroom after separating from Marilyn (the couple remained close even after divorcing in 1979). Worse yet, Carl began using cocaine and

Stephen Love was fired for taking more than his fair share from the CBS deal. It was the Beach Boys' lowest point yet, highlighted by onstage and backstage squabbling during a tour of Australia and New Zealand. To top things off, Dennis's 1977 album, *Pacific Ocean Blue*, was a commercial and critical success, and the rest of the band resented him for it.

The group ended the seventies with two lackluster releases, 1978's *The M.I.U. Album* and 1979's *L.A. (Light Album)*. Although Bruce rejoined the band to help out with *L.A.*, neither LP was a hit. Their 1980 follow-up, *Keepin' the Summer Alive*, fared even worse. There didn't seem to be much reason for the Beach Boys to go on.

85

ENDLESS HARMONY

The Beach Boys' best years were behind them by the early '80s. *Keepin' the Summer Alive* had barely dented the top 100, and Carl left the group to work on his well-received solo albums, *Carl Wilson* and *Youngblood*. Mike divorced and remarried again, and released a solo album of his own called *Looking Back with Love*.

Brian remained isolated under the watchful eyes of Stanley Love and Rocky Pamplin, and was briefly institutionalized after a weeklong binge in Mexico and San Diego. Dennis drifted steadily toward disaster.

The group recorded only a few more albums together in the coming years, but while their music never again reached the heights of *Pet Sounds* or "Good Vibrations," they still had a few surprises—and hits—left in them. Sadly, things got a lot worse before they got any better.

"Sail On, Sailor"

After the triumph of *Pacific Ocean Blue*, Dennis's life went downhill fast. He and Barbara had long since divorced, and he began a long and stormy relationship with a beautiful actress named Karen Lamm; they were married in 1976. Karen's fiery temperament was a good match for Dennis's, and the two shared a love for partying. But while Karen knew her limits and eventually stopped abusing drugs, Dennis never lost his taste for them and began using heroin. When he

Brian and Carl Wilson during the 1986 shoot for a video of the song "California Dreamin'"

became abusive, Karen left him and they divorced in 1980. He then began an affair with Christine McVie of the band Fleetwood Mac.

His true love throughout these troubled years, however, was his boat the *Harmony*. He loved to sail it up and down the Pacific coast, or just hang out on it at Marina Del Rey where it was moored. But the boat was repossessed by a bank in 1981, and Dennis—whose income was absorbed by drugs and alcohol—was unable to buy it back. He was heartbroken.

Dennis was urged by the concerned Beach Boys to seek professional help for his addictions, but he resisted. He considered approaching Eugene Landy, Brian's one-time savior, but never followed through. His downward spiral continued, and in 1983 he married for the final time. He and his young wife, Shawn, soon had a son named Gage, whom Dennis adored. Still, the couple soon separated. Dennis began spending a lot of time on the boat of a friend, across from the slip in which the *Harmony* had once been docked. On the afternoon of December 28, 1983, Dennis Wilson drowned while swimming in

Dennis Wilson, Dreamer

Despite Brian's celebrated musical genius, it was the middle Wilson brother who provided the Beach Boys with their inspiration. "I remember Brian would drill Dennis on what was going on, really pump him for the [surfing] terminology and the newest thing," their brother Carl recalled in a 1983 interview. "Dennis was the embodiment of the group; he lived what we were singing about . . . I mean, we could have gotten it from magazines like everyone else did. Dennis was out there doing it."

Dennis was also the only Beach Boy to try his hand at acting. He starred opposite folk rocker James Taylor in director Monte Hellman's 1971 *Two-Lane Blacktop*, playing a character known only as "the Mechanic." Even though the film became a critical favorite and cult classic, it wasn't a satisfying experience for Dennis, and he never made another feature film.

He turned his attention instead to solo work. Dennis wrote and recorded *Pacific Ocean Blue* throughout 1976 and early 1977, and began an abandoned follow-up, *Bamboo*, late in 1977. *Pacific Ocean Blue* was a hit with critics and record buyers alike, and it is generally considered the era's best Beach Boys–related release. A review in *Rolling Stone* magazine said that Dennis's songs "have a way of taking hold of your emotions"—or, as Carl put it, he "made it true."

the frigid waters of Marina Del Rey. He was only thirty-nine years old.

Brian Gets Back on Track

While Dennis's life was crumbling, Brian was finally managing to get a grip on his. It wasn't easy. After several stays in local hospitals, it was clear that Brian needed Dr. Landy's help again. Marilyn dismissed Stan and Rocky and convinced the other Beach Boys to rehire the psychologist. They reluctantly agreed and "fired" Brian from the band in an effort to keep his income from Carolyn Williams, a live-in nurse who had been supplying him with junk food, liquor, and drugs. Landy then whisked Brian away to a remote house in Hawaii for a three-month rest.

Brian was dangerously out of shape, and the exercise program and diet Landy and his staff put him on was grueling. But he began losing weight and regaining his self-respect, and he began to play and write music again. Brian also faced the inner demons that had plagued him since his childhood: "I'd spent years ignoring these emotions, drowning them in booze, drugs, and food," he later wrote in his autobiography. "There was none of that anymore." In March 1983, he held a press conference at Honolulu's Kahala Hilton Hotel to dispel rumors that Landy had kidnapped him. Brian, who was usually terrified of such events, conducted himself with dignity. Soon after, he returned home a slimmer and saner man, ready to face the Beach Boys.

Picking Up the Pieces

With the unwanted (except by Brian) assistance of Eugene Landy, the group began rehearsing together shortly before Dennis's death. The sessions were tense and not very productive, but Brian was better able to assert himself in the band. They were scheduled to play a Fourth of July concert in Washington, D.C., but Secretary of the Interior James Watt banned their appearance, believing that they would attract "the wrong element." President Ronald Reagan, a Beach Boys fan, scolded Watt and invited the group to the White House later that month.

Dennis's passing late in the year devastated both Brian and Carl. They carried on as best as they could, and pulled a few strings with President Reagan to help arrange Dennis's burial at sea. (Such services were normally against federal law.) It was a fitting farewell for the man who had inspired the Beach Boys.

The remaining band members continued to tour, and Brian occasionally joined them onstage. He and Landy had been in touch with English record producer Steve Levine, famous for producing the Culture Club, and in the fall of 1984 the group flew to London to record an album with him. It was a difficult experience for all of them. Levine's rigorous studio methods bothered Brian, and the rest of the Beach Boys were irritated by Landy's presence and his suggestions about the lyrics to their songs. The album was released in 1985. Titled simply *The Beach Boys*, it was a surprising success and reached number fifty-two on the charts. A nostalgic single, "Getcha Back," peaked at number twenty-six. *The Beach Boys* would be the final full album of original songs from the group, as well as their last for CBS: The label didn't renew their contract when it expired in 1985.

One Last Comeback

As usual, the next few years were full of ups and downs for the band. Brian began working on a solo album with Eugene Landy, and, in January 1988, the Beach Boys were inducted into the Rock and Roll Hall of Fame. They received a standing ovation at the ceremony,

Fun Fact!

Brian Wilson not only writes songs, he has songs written about him. The Barenaked Ladies composed a tune called "Brian Wilson," and British band Tears for Fears wrote a song called "Brian Wilson Said."

Mike Love opened the Club Kokomo restaurant and nightclub in Anaheim, California. It was named after the Beach Boys' 1988 hit, "Kokomo."

and in a moving acceptance speech Brian said, "I only wish my younger brother Dennis could be at our side tonight." Unfortunately, Mike stole the spotlight with a long and bitter rant directed at some of rock and roll's greatest musicians—many of whom were in the audience. He also criticized other artists, such as Diana Ross and Paul McCartney, for not attending the induction ceremony.

The group bounced back from this embarrassment that summer with "Kokomo," a contribution to the sound track for the Tom Cruise movie *Cocktail.* This surprise hit song, which was written and recorded without Brian, became the first Beach Boys record to reach number one since "Good Vibrations." Capitol released an album in 1989 to capitalize on its unexpected success. Composed of leftover material, different versions of older songs, and even a new tune from Brian called "In My Car," *Still Cruisin'* was neither a popular nor critical success. Brian's solo project, *Brian Wilson,* was also released around the time that "Kokomo" came out. His amazing mental and physical

The Beach Boys' 1988 hit "Kokomo" helped them stage a comeback.

comeback was praised more than the album itself, which nevertheless sold respectably and broke into the top 100.

The new decade saw the end of the Beach Boys' recording career. A final album, 1992's *Summer in Paradise,* came out under the group's name, but it was a CD-only release on which Brian played no part. He officially left the band when the other members filed a lawsuit alleging he'd withheld money from them over the years. He also published his best-selling autobiography with co-author Todd Gold during this period, and its unflattering portrait of his band mates sparked controversy. Charges that Eugene Landy had actually written the book led Brian to distance himself from the psychologist in the interest of his career. The Beach Boys remained a successful live act even without their founder, but they were all soon devastated by another tragedy: On February 6, 1998, Carl Wilson died of lung cancer at the age of fifty-one.

Although deeply shaken, Mike, Al, and Bruce continued to perform together for a time. They soon drifted apart, however, and by 2001 Mike

Love was the only original member left in the
band calling itself the Beach Boys.

"And Your Dream Comes True"

Against the odds, Brian Wilson outlived both his
younger brothers and the troubled times that
nearly cost him his own life. He managed to stay
fit and drug-free after leaving Dr. Landy's care
for good, and even started a second family in
1995 with his new wife, Melinda Ledbetter.

Brian's persistence has paid off in the past few
years. He was the subject of a successful
documentary called *I Just Wasn't Made for These
Times* in 1995, while many considered his 1998
album, *Imagination,* a worthy follow-up to *Pet
Sounds.* In 2000, Brian was inducted into the
Songwriter's Hall of Fame, where former Beatle
Paul McCartney thanked him "for having that
'thing' you can do with your music. You just put
those notes and those harmonies together, stick a
couple of words over the top of it, and you've got
me, any day." In March 2001, he was honored
with an all-star tribute at New York City's

Radio City Music Hall. Performers like Elton
John, the Harlem Boys Choir, and Brian's
daughters Carnie and Wendy—who had achieved
their own musical success as part of the trio
Wilson Phillips in the early '90s—gathered to
sing his praises and perform his music. The gala
was broadcast on the TNT network on July 4,
2001. That same season, Brian toured the United
States with fellow '60s musical icon Paul Simon
in a series of sold-out performances that left fans
wanting more.

Perhaps best of all, Brian lived to see the one-
of-a-kind music he made with his brothers, their
cousin, and a high school friend become an
enduring part of rock and roll history. Through
him, the Beach Boys live on.

SELECTED DISCOGRAPHY

1962 *Surfin' Safari*

1963 *Surfer Girl*

1964 *Shut Down Volume 2*

1965 *The Beach Boys Today!*

1965 *Summer Days (And Summer Nights!!)*

1966 *Pet Sounds*

1967 *Smiley Smile*

1967 *Wild Honey*

1968 *Friends*

1969 *20/20*

1970 *Sunflower*

1971 *Surf's Up*

1973 *Holland*

1976 *15 Big Ones*

1977 *The Beach Boys Love You*

1979 *L.A. (Light Album)*

1985 *The Beach Boys*

1992 *Summer in Paradise*

GLOSSARY

A&R Short for "artist and repertoire"; in a record company, the department responsible for finding, signing, and developing new musical acts.

avant-garde Of or relating to new or experimental concepts, especially in the arts.

balk To refuse abruptly.

barbershop quartet Four-member vocal group that sings popular, unaccompanied songs in close harmony. Named for the early twentieth century American custom of men forming impromptu singing groups in barbershops.

counterculture Culture whose values are opposed to those of established society, such as the hippie movement of the late 1960s.

demeaning Lowering in status or reputation; insulting.

dispel To drive away or scatter.

estrangement The breaking of a bond of loyalty or affection.

fledgling Person who is new to or inexperienced in something.

incessant Continuing without interruption.

languish To suffer neglect.

makeshift Temporary or substitutional, as in a situation or facility.

overdubbing Recording music over other musical tracks to create a combined or layered sound.

persistent Continuing on a course in spite of interference.

phonograph Record player.

rant To talk in a noisy, excited manner.

renowned Widely acclaimed and highly honored; famous.

resilience Ability to recover from or adjust to changes or hardships.

reverb Electronically produced echo effect.

sparse Of few and scattered elements.

Rock and Roll Hall of Fame Foundation
1290 Avenue of the Americas
New York, NY 10104

Rock and Roll Hall of Fame and Museum
One Key Plaza
Cleveland, OH 44114
(888) 764-ROCK (7625)
Web site: http://www.rockhall.com

Web Sites

Due to the changing nature of Internet links, the Rosen Publishing Group, Inc., has developed an online list of Web sites related to the subject of this book. This site is updated regularly. Please use this link to access the list:

http://www.rosenlinks.com/rrhf/bebo/

FOR FURTHER READING

Gaines, Steven. *Heroes and Villains: The True Story of the Beach Boys.* New York: New American Library, 1986.

White, Timothy. *The Nearest Faraway Place: Brian Wilson, the Beach Boys and the Southern California Experience.* New York: Henry Holt and Company, 1994.

Wilson, Brian. *Wouldn't It Be Nice: My Own Story.* New York: HarperCollins, 1991.

Works Cited

Doggett, Peter. "The Beach Boys." *Record Collector,* September 1990.

Gaines, Steven. *Heroes and Villains: The True Story of the Beach Boys.* New York: New American Library, 1986.

Himes, Geoffrey. "High Times and Ebb Tides." *Musician,* September 1983.

Leaf, David. *The Beach Boys.* Philadelphia: Courage Books, 1985.

Vineyard, Jennifer. "Beatle Honors Beach Boy at Songwriters' Hall of Fame." *Rolling Stone.com,* June 17, 2000.

Webb, Adam. *Dumb Angel: The Life and Music of Dennis Wilson.* London: Creation Books, 2001.

Wilson, Brian. *Wouldn't It Be Nice: My Own Story.* New York: HarperCollins, 1991.

INDEX

Index

About the Author

Mark Holcomb is a freelance writer who lives in Brooklyn, New York. His work has appeared in *The Village Voice, Film Quarterly,* and *indieWIRE.*

Photo Credits

Cover, pp. 5, 7, 9, 23, 28, 34, 71, 82, 86, 88 © Corbis; pp. 4, 20, 32, 39, 42, 45, 48, 56, 74 © Hulton Archive; pp. 12, 16–17, 66, 69, 96, 98–99 © AP/Wide World Photos; pp. 59, 79 by Nelson Sá.

Editor

Eliza Berkowitz

Design

Thomas Forget

Layout

Nelson Sá